REPTILES
and
AMPHIBIANS

Troll Associates

REPTILES
and
AMPHIBIANS

by Louis Sabin

Illustrated by Nancy Zink-White

Troll Associates

Library of Congress Cataloging in Publication Data

Sabin, Louis.
   Reptiles and amphibians.

   Summary: Describes the physical characteristics,
habits, and natural environment of various species of
reptiles and amphibians.
   1. Reptiles—Juvenile literature. 2. Amphibians—
Juvenile literature. [1. Reptiles. 2. Amphibians]
I. Zink-White, Nancy, ill. II. Title.
QL644.2.S23   1985   597.6   84-8445
ISBN 0-8167-0294-2 (lib. bdg.)
ISBN 0-8167-0295-0 (pbk.)

Many millions of years ago, before there were birds flying through the air, and before there were animals walking over the land, a strange creature crawled out of the water. In many ways it was like a fish. But it had one very important difference: it breathed air. Even so, it spent much of its time in the water, and it laid its eggs there, too.

This creature was the first amphibian. *Amphibian* means "double life," a name given this form of life because it could exist in water and on land. Today's descendants of these long-ago amphibians are the frog, the toad, the salamander, and the newt.

Newt

Toad

Frog

Salamander

Those first animals that left the water are also the ancestors of another form of life called reptiles. The reptile family includes snakes, lizards, turtles, crocodiles, and alligators.

Some reptiles and amphibians look very much alike. But there are several ways to tell

them apart. All reptiles have scaly skin that feels dry to the touch, but amphibians have smooth, moist skin. Reptiles have claws at the ends of their toes, but amphibians have soft pads on their toes. And reptiles lay their eggs on land, while amphibians lay their eggs in the water.

Still, in many ways reptiles and amphibians are very much alike. Both are cold-blooded animals. This means they cannot keep a constant body temperature. When a reptile or amphibian is in a very hot place, its body temperature zooms way up. If it is in a very cold place, its body temperature drops very low.

If its body temperature is too high or too low, a reptile or amphibian cannot live a normal life. So these animals move from place to place to keep their bodies at the right temperature—about 70 to 80 degrees Fahrenheit. They bask in sunlight to warm themselves and move beneath a rock or underground or into water to cool themselves.

Reptiles and amphibians that live in places with very cold winters usually hibernate. That is, they burrow underground, below the frost line, and sleep until spring brings warmth again.

Before this long sleep begins, however, the cold-blooded animals eat a lot of food. Their bodies will use this food while the animals hibernate. If you were to see a hibernating reptile or amphibian, you might think it is dead. You could turn it upside down or sideways, and it would stay just as you placed it. A hibernating snake or toad doesn't even seem to be breathing.

Reptiles and amphibians live every place on Earth except where the ground is frozen all year round. In those frozen places they would not survive, because they would not be able to keep their body temperatures above freezing.

Long ago, when the climate was warm all over the world, reptiles ruled the Earth. There were many different kinds of reptiles, both small and large. The largest were the dinosaurs, or "terrible lizards." But there are no dinosaurs today. In fact, of the many different groups of reptiles that lived long ago, only four remain.

The lizards and snakes make up one group. Alligators and crocodiles and their relatives make up the second group. The turtles are in the third group. And the fourth group contains only the tuatara.

The tuatara is a lizardlike reptile that is found only in New Zealand. It is the last surviving member of a group of beak-headed reptiles that lived millions of years ago. This two-foot-long creature even looks something like a small dinosaur.

Alligators and crocodiles are reptiles that have tough, scaly hides, long tails, and powerful jaws. You can tell a crocodile from an alligator by looking at the jaws. The alligator's jaw is broad and rounded, while the crocodile's is long and pointed.

All the members of this group of reptiles—called crocodilians—are good swimmers. They are found in warm climates, where they spend much of their time in the water. But they come out of the water to lay their eggs on land.

Crocodilians are carnivores, or meat-eaters. The adults generally feed on fish, shellfish, birds, and other small animals. They protect themselves by diving under-water or by using their strong jaws and sharp teeth.

Alligator   *Crocodile*

The turtle, which is toothless, does not usually fight back. Except for the snapping turtle, which bites, most turtles just withdraw into their hard shells or hide in shrubbery or under the water.

There are about 250 kinds of turtles, ranging from tiny ones to the huge leatherback turtle that is the size of a small car. There are turtles that live on land all the time, turtles that spend part of the time in ponds and streams, and turtles that live all their lives in water. All turtles, however,

18

lay their eggs on land. And all turtles breathe air—even those that live in the ocean.

Ocean turtles eat seaweed, jellyfish, and shellfish. Freshwater turtles eat plants, insects, shellfish, fish, frogs, and other foods. Land turtles also eat plants, insects, and small animals.

The turtle is different from all other reptiles because it has a shell. This shell is actually part of the turtle's skeleton!

There are more than 2,000 kinds of snakes in the world, but most of them are not poisonous and are not dangerous to humans. The snake sheds its scaly skin several times a year as it grows. This is called molting. Most snakes lay eggs, although a few kinds of snakes give birth to living young.

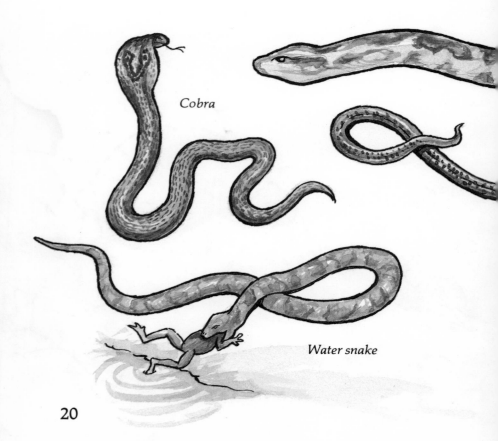

Cobra

Water snake

Snakes are not plant-eaters. The green snake eats insects. The water snake eats fish and frogs. The garter snake hunts for worms, fish, rodents, and birds. Large snakes, like the python, can eat large animals.

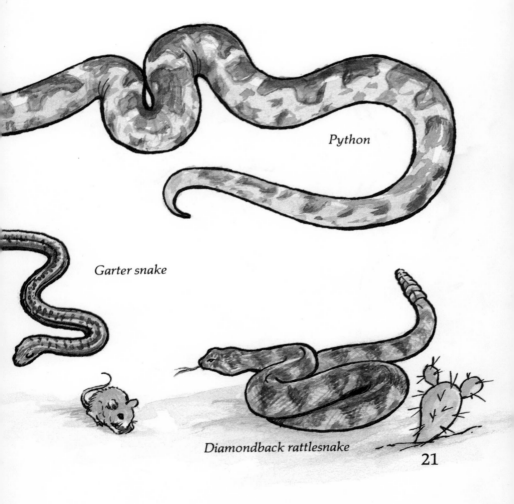

Python

Garter snake

Diamondback rattlesnake

Because they have no legs, snakes must slither or slide from one place to another. Different snakes move in different ways. Black snakes slide over the ground in wavy curves. Sidewinder snakes get their name because they travel in wide, looping moves from side to side. Most vipers pull the front part of the body forward, then follow it with the rest of the body in up-and-down waves.

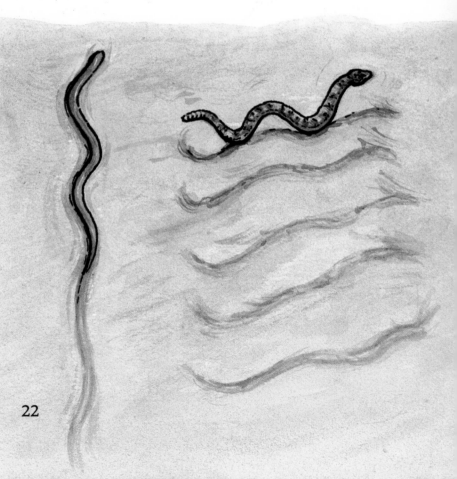

The tree boa wraps itself around a tree trunk. Then it stretches its front part upward, grips the trunk with the scales behind its head, and pulls up the rest of the body.

When they sense danger, snakes usually retreat to their homes in the ground, under rocks, or up a tree. But if cornered, they will fight back. Some snakes can spit poison. Some have a poisonous bite. And some crush their enemies.

24

Komodo dragon

Lizards are closely related to snakes. The largest lizard known, the Komodo dragon of Southeast Asia, is about ten feet long. The smallest lizards are only about two inches in length.

Nearly all lizards have a short body, a long tail, and four legs. Two-legged and legless lizards exist, but they are rare. Like snakes, all lizards shed their skin. Most lizards eat insects, catching them as they fly past. But the horned lizard, also called the horned toad, usually eats ants, and the Komodo dragon eats small animals. There are also lizards that eat seaweed, and some that like plants or fruit.

Different species of lizards live in different types of homes. Many, such as the desert lizards, live underground and in cracks between rocks. Others, such as the anole and the chameleon, live in trees. These tree lizards have the ability to change colors to match their surroundings. That is their best form of defense against enemies.

Chameleon

26

Gila monster

All lizards have teeth, and many of these animals will bite when they are threatened. But only the Gila monster and the beaded lizard are poisonous.

Salamanders and newts, which look very much like lizards, are not reptiles. They are amphibians. They have a moist slimy skin and no claws.

And, like all amphibians, they develop differently from reptiles. In common with frogs and toads, the salamander and newt are tadpoles when they first hatch from their eggs. As tadpoles, they have fins for swimming and gills for breathing. Then, in a series of changes, called metamorphosis, they turn into salamanders and newts. The gills and fins are gone, but they now have four legs, and lungs for breathing air.

Frogs and toads are very much alike, although there are differences between them. Both lay eggs in water, but frog eggs are laid in a cluster; while toad eggs are laid in a string.

The frog has a smooth, moist skin; but the toad has a dry, bumpy skin. The frog leaps and jumps; while the toad walks or hops.

The frog is usually slim and has a long, narrow head; but the toad has a pudgy body and a short, wide head. Frogs live in or near water all the time. Toads, however, spend more time on dry land.

All amphibians eat insects and worms and other very small creatures. Surprisingly, amphibians do not drink water. Instead, they absorb it through their skin. Amphibians are mostly defenseless. They protect themselves by not moving, by blending with their surroundings, by diving underwater, or by playing dead.

Like all other living things, reptiles and amphibians play an important role in the web of life. And they are among the most fascinating creatures on Earth.